MW00773222

"WEARING THE CAPTAIN'S GOWN"

By Gene Yontz

Copyright© 2018 Gene Yontz

i

Three of my favorite people have passed away during the writing of this book. Kent Young, Aunt Donna, and Uncle Jim. Miss you very much.

ISBN: 978-1-62249-439-2

Published by
The Educational Publisher Inc.
Biblio Publishing
BiblioPublishing.com
Columbus, Ohio

Table of Contents

Introduction

I taught school for thirty-one years before retiring on March 1, 2012. In 1984, I began taking notes about funny and special moments that happened during my teaching career. This book contains quotes and responses to questions my students have made over the years. I have written stories that have a funny side, but a few are serious in nature.

Writing this book was a bucket list item for me and I found it to be more difficult than expected. There are seventy-six stories in this book which are true, but one story is fiction. As you are reading, try to determine which story is not true. There will be a time when I will ask you for your selection of the fictional story.

The 1975 World Champion Cincinnati Reds had the "Great Eight" which included: Pete Rose, Joe Morgan, Ken Griffey, George Foster, Johnny Bench, Tony Perez, Dave Concepcion, and Cesar Geronimo. Well I have my "Great Eight" which includes Gene Yontz (Dad), Edith Yontz (Mom), Rick Yontz, Randy Yontz, Craig Yontz, Terry Yontz, Nicholas Yontz, and Ashley Yontz. I hope you enjoy the read.

I would like to give a special shout out to my daughter Ashley for typing the book. You are the best. Thank you very much. Love, Dad.

<u>One</u> <u>Liners</u>

"I can't wait to graduate and wear the captain's gown."

Education

Water Balloons

What a crew!

It was the last day of school in May of 1999. A field day is held at the conclusion of each school year. We received a heads up about a possible water balloon fight between the kids. We confiscated all of the water balloons as the kids

Short Answer

What pope preceded Pope Benedict XVI?
Correct Answer: Pope John Paul
Student Answer: "Pope John Paul Jones"

entered the building in the morning. The kids were not happy, but that's the way it goes.

It was a beautiful day and all of the events went well. At the conclusion of the day, we gathered all of the students together for one final time.

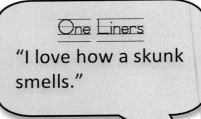

One Liners

"I love how a skunk smells."

While the kids were being assembled, three teachers took all of those water balloons we collected up on the roof. When the kids were within range, those teachers bombed the rugrats that were below. Funniest thing I've ever seen! After school hours, the staff and kids had a huge shaving cream fight. We all had fun.

Field Day

The time period was the early 1990's. It was the last week of school for a student teacher. The sky was full of sun and the kids were enjoying a field day. An 8th grade boy decided he would catch a few rays on a slide. He took his shirt off and positioned himself lying on his back at the top of the slide with his arms behind his head.

The whistle blows for the kids to line up and go inside. This boy had lodged his arms in the railing and was stuck. There were numerous attempts to remove this boy from his agony, but nothing worked. In the end, the fire department was called in and disassembled the slide removing the student. Reminds me of Flick in The Christmas Story.

Kindergarten

A friend of mine is an elementary physical education teacher. He has twenty-eight years of experience. He wanted me to share this story with you.

At the beginning of each school year, the teacher should discuss the rules and expectations for each class. This teacher begins day

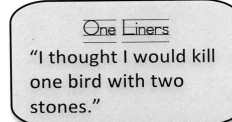

one with a kindergarten class. He instructs the little ones on what to wear to school on days they have gym class.

Trying to share a little humor with the class, my friend said, "Girls you probably shouldn't wear a dress or skirt and that goes for you too boys."

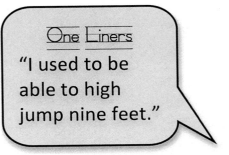

A 5-year-old boy responds, "What do you think we are, a bunch of F******?" Incredible!

Retaliation

I arrived at school at 6:45am and parked toward the back of the building. I would cut through the gym to get to my

5

Gene Yontz

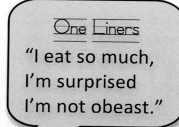

One Liners

"I eat so much, I'm surprised I'm not obeast."

classroom. The custodian would sweep the gym floor before school and leave his broom under a stairwell. There were times I would take the broom and hide it. It didn't take long for him to figure out what was going on. I was waiting for retaliation on his part.

I was teaching a morning class and the custodian entered my room unannounced. I knew something was up because he never showed his face in my classroom. I'm near my desk as he entered my room. He had his hands in his pockets. He had planted a fart machine in my desk and had the controls in his pocket. He activated the machine to "thunderous" applause from my students. It was hilarious!

Mr. Mendenhall

I was in my first year of teaching at Indian Valley Middle School. Mr. Mendenhall was the assistant principal. He was quite a character. A very interesting individual with a tremendous imagination.

Short Answer

What do you think is going to happen?
Student Answer: "I don't know. It depends upon the future."

I was in the middle of teaching a class full of 8th graders. One of the students in the back near the door raised his hand. I called on him. He told me he thinks there is a cat outside

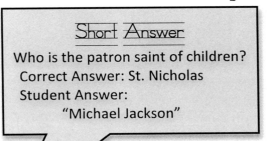

Short Answer

Who is the patron saint of children?
Correct Answer: St. Nicholas
Student Answer:
"Michael Jackson"

the door. He heard meowing and scratching at the bottom of the door. I went to check it out. I heard what the student heard. I opened the door and there was Mr. Mendenhall down on all fours scratching the door with his fingernails, and meowing his heart away.

I loved my years teaching at Indian Valley.

Halloween

I hate Halloween. Every year it rolls around the kids get dressed up and it becomes such a distraction. I can never get anything accomplished on that day.

I am sixty-three years old and have only dressed up one time while teaching. A friend called me up the night before and asked if I would dress up.

I said, "Absolutely not."

After about five minutes of persuasion, I agreed. My friend was in the Air National Guard. My job was to wear his boots and bottom fatigues. He wore his shirt and cap. We went as an upper and lower G.I.

Gene Yontz

Adam's Apple

In 1985, I was teaching an 8th grade social studies class. I forget the question I asked, but I remember the response I was searching for, "Adam's apple". After a series of incorrect answers, I started giving clues. My first clue was "this man's name was found in the Bible." No response. My second clue was "this is part of a man's body." A hand went up immediately in the back of the room. I called on Tim.

He said, "Peter."

One Liners

I told the class that Mount Everest is in Nepal. A student replied, "What's it doing over there?"

Every student in the room cracked up. I was laughing on the inside but had to keep my composure. I took Tim out in the hallway, which appeared to the kids that disciplinary action was going to be applied.

I said, "Tim, that was the funniest damn thing I have ever heard. But, I need you to go back in there with a frown on your face."

It is now 2018 and the two of us still laugh about it.

Expecting

It was my initial year at Indian Valley Middle School. We were pregnant with our first born, Nicholas. The principal made an announcement there would be a brief meeting after school.

The school day concluded and I headed toward the library. I entered the room and noticed many wrapped packages. I thought to myself, did I miss something? It turned out to be a baby shower for me. I still have the growth measuring board they gave me. It is a priceless possession.

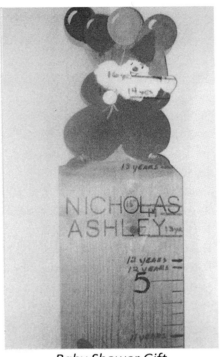

Baby Shower Gift

Tables Turned

One of my friends is the biggest practical joker I know. Well the time had come to put the shoe on the other foot.

Our school nurse had an idea that turned out to be brilliant. She put out a directive that all school employees were required to give a urine sample ordered by the superintendent.

Gene Yontz

My friend asked me, "Are you going to comply?"

I said, "Sure."

He replied, "I'm not going to because I think it's a joke."
As the school day progressed, my friend told me he turned in his sample and it contained Mountain Dew.
I said, "I don't know if you should have done that. I think this thing is on the up and up."
It is now in the afternoon. My friend began to question his Mountain Dew decision and submitted an authentic urine sample.

At the end of the teaching day, the principal called for a short meeting in the library. Everyone filed in. The principal thanked Mr. Norris for being the only person to comply with the directive. April Fools! It was a classic!

<u>One Liners</u>
I asked this girl, "Do you kiss your boyfriend after you eat those Flaming Hot Cheetos?" She replied, "He doesn't mind, he's from Mexico."

<u>Short Answer</u>
Who is Jessie Jackson?
    Correct Answer: civil rights activist
    Student Answer: "Ain't he one of the Jackson Five?"

One Liners

"In horse racing, bet on the long shot. You'll only win one out of ten times, but at least you'll have a fifty-fifty chance."

History Humor

If you attended middle school before 1990, you probably remember film strips. I was teaching an 8th grade history class this particular day. Ninety-nine percent of the time, I would preview the film strip to address the important points. This time I didn't and the following happened. Everything was going well until I hear, "When General Cornwallis beat off the troops at Yorktown." The kids laughed and so did I. At least they were paying attention.

Lawnmower

Some of my students took their academic classes in the morning and worked a small job in the afternoon. Many of my students needed spending money. This particular young man, the same one that wanted to "poke a dead body with a stick", worked for the school mowing grass. I received a phone call from a teacher

One Liners

"Did the beaver see his shadow on Groundhog Day?"

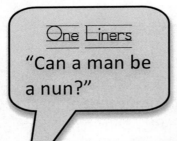

One Liners

"Can a man be a nun?"

telling me that she saw the student dancing with a lawnmower.

I said "What kind of dance is he doing?"

She replied, "What?" and hung up.

Some people have no sense of humor!

Tree Crew

One of my students only had one semester to graduate from high school. He informed me he was going to drop out and join a tree crew to make some money. I literally begged him not to do this, but he went ahead with it.

Five years later, I ran into him at a local gas station. We exchanged pleasantries and he told me he had a son and named him after himself.

One Liners

"There are catfish in the Ohio River that are bigger than us."

I said "You named your son, D*** A**?"
We both laughed, me more than him.

Watergate

I was beginning a lesson about the Watergate scandal. I asked the class if any of them knew anything about this part of our history. Not many hands went up, but I was surprised this one boy wanted to respond. I called upon him and I said, "Have at it."

He started off well, explaining about the break-in at the Watergate Hotel. He talked about the reporting of Carl Bernstein and Bob Woodward of the Washington Post. The names of G. Gordon Liddy, Richard Nixon and Deep Throat were also mentioned. He knew President Nixon resigned in August of 1974.

I was very impressed with his knowledge on this topic. He concluded with, "And then Harrison Ford pardoned Richard Nixon."

One Liners

"Is Easter on Sunday this year?"

Turkeys

In the 1970's, a guidance counselor at a local high school printed up certificates stating new teachers would receive a free Christmas turkey, redeemable at a local grocery store. He placed the certificates in the rookie teachers' mailboxes on the last day prior to Christmas break.

A few of the innocent people tried to place their order. Obviously, not one order was filled. When the teachers returned from Christmas break they began to ask questions. They were informed this had become a tradition. Not too many people knew who was the prankster, but I did.

13

<u>Short</u> <u>Answers</u>

What is the 19th Amendment?
  Correct Answer: Gave women the right to
    vote
  Student Answer: "Thou shall not kill."

Recruiting

A friend of mine was a guidance counselor at the local joint vocational school. Part of his duties were to visit high schools in the county and recruit students to attend J.V.S. He would explain the courses and programs offered for the following year.

This particular day he was visiting an alternative school. This was probably the final stop for many of the kids. My friend entered the classroom and introduced himself to the classroom teacher. The next words spoken in that classroom came from a student in the second row.

He said, "What's that M--- F--- doing here?"

The classroom teacher just shrugged his shoulders and the guidance counselor proceeded. Unbelievable!

<u>One</u> <u>Liners</u>

"Whoever thought of the Ten Commandments was a smart man."

Lunch at Wendy's

The last few years of my teaching career I taught C.B.I. (Career Based Intervention). The students would attend academic classes in the morning and work a job in the afternoon.

One of my favorite students was Mark. He worked at Wendy's during the lunch shift. I met with Mark at Wendy's to talk about a few things before he went on the clock. Mark ordered a chicken sandwich. I settled for some type of salad.

> ### One Liners
>
> A male student wore a kilt to school and was sent home. A student responded, "You can't send a kid home because of his religion."

It was winter and I remember it being quite cold that day. Mark and I just sat down to eat and he saw someone in the parking lot that needed help. He told me he would be right back. Shortly after Mark left the table, a woman sat down in Mark's seat and began to eat his sandwich. Obviously, I was surprised. I immediately thought a practical joke was being played on me, so I didn't react.

After a few minutes had passed, she was still eating Mark's sandwich.

I said to her, "That's Mark's sandwich."

> ### One Liners
>
> "Didn't the Virgin Mary eat the fruit?"

She didn't respond, just kept chomping away. A few more minutes passed and Mark returned to the table. He had a stunned look on his face and said, "What's going on?"

> One Liners
>
> "Man, I was close. I was only off a lot."

I said, "Do you know her?"

He said, "No, do you know her?"

I said, "No!"

Bottom line, this lady came in from off the street. She was dressed in warm clothes and didn't look like she had missed many meals. Before she was removed from the restaurant, she asked me if I was going to finish my salad.

Sunday School

Some of my friends attended Sunday school at a church in central Ohio. They were approximately in the 6th grade. The minister gave the kids an assignment. The kids were to memorize the names of the books in the Bible. They were given two weeks to get this done.

> One Liners
>
> "They test three people a week for a urine example."

The time had come for the gang to divulge their knowledge of the titles. The minister called on Ray who wasn't

16

the most diligent student.
Ray began with, "Matthew, Mark, Luke, and John went to bed with their britches on." The minister saw no humor in Ray's response. Ray's buddies did.

Tommy

I was teaching a sophomore class at a local high school in 2002. I had a great rapport with this student, we'll call him Tommy. We teased each other quite a bit, but nobody got hurt.

My principal was a great guy. He cared about the kids and liked to have fun. He agreed to help me play a joke on Tommy. I handed Mr. Vanuch the script to read.
Mr. Vanuch called into my room at 10:20am and said, "Mr. Yontz, is Tommy there?"

I replied, "He's sitting right in front of me."

He said, "His mother called and had a few messages for him."

I said, "Go ahead."

Mr. Vanuch began to read from the script. He said, "Tell Tommy his ballet lesson has been cancelled for today. His Scooby Doo underwear is in at JC Penney's and his Victoria Secret catalogue application has been

One Liners

"This is a joint vacational school."

Gene Yontz

denied because he is underage."

It was great! Entire class laughed and so did Tommy. His mom also thought it was funny. I wish all of the parents had a sense of humor like hers.

Homework

I've always believed that if a student completed an assignment, it was my obligation to give it a grade. A student in my class told me he knew a teacher that would sometimes put a grade on a paper without looking at it. He also said he could prove it.
I said, "Okay, Prove it."

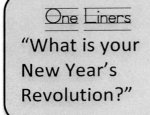

One Liners
"What is your New Year's Revolution?"

The kids were working on an assignment in class. This boy had written a letter to his girlfriend along with the completed assignment. At the conclusion of the period, the teacher walked around the room and collected the papers. The teacher mistakenly picked up the boy's letter to his girlfriend. When his letter was returned, the student had received seven out of ten points. SAD!!!

Short Answers
What do you know about the Garden of Eden?
Student Answer: "Mary and the rest of them were in there naked."

Orchestra Class

My planning period was at the end of the day. Because of overcrowding, my classroom was used for a small orchestra class. I was allowed to stay in the room if I chose. Some days I did, some I didn't. This happened one day I stayed.

I was sitting at my desk working on a few things. After warm ups, the group started to play a song they had been working on for some time. I noticed the instructor was becoming increasingly frustrated. After about a minute into the song, the instructor began waving his arms and stopped everyone from playing. He then pointed to a boy and said, "You are a beat off."

One Liners

A high school basketball coach was talking to his players about improving their work "ethnic".

One Liners

A high school principal referred to something crazy happening as "lucradous".

The instructor was a well-liked, retired marching band director. I believe he was teaching this class to stay active and for his love of music. This wonderful gentleman has passed. R.I.P.

Gene Yontz

Buzzy

The location was Crawfordsville, Indiana. Ms. Russell was teaching a kindergarten class full of five year olds. One of her students, I will call him "Buzzy", had a problem with authority. Every time Buzzy was challenged by Ms. Russell, he would call her the "B" word. There were numerous conversations with Buzzy and his parents about the situation. Nothing seemed to work. Just by chance one day Ms. Russell picked up Buzzy and put him on her lap. Their relationship changed dramatically. Anytime Buzzy was positioned on Ms. Russell's lap the "B" word was not used.

> One Liners
>
> "Give me a pacific restaurant."

There was a vast improvement between teacher and student. Ms. Russell had Buzzy on her lap and noticed he had something in his mouth.

Ms. Russell asked, "What do you have in your mouth?"

He reached into his mouth and pulled out a wad of tobacco.

"Where did you get that Buzzy?" she said.

Buzzy replied, "On the sidewalk outside of school."

Skyscootus

The year was 1960. The location was 2015 Redleaf Drive in Louisville, Kentucky. I was six years old and visiting my Aunt June and Uncle Bob. Behind their residence was a large cornfield. My uncle told me to never go in the cornfield because the "skyscootus" would get me. It was his way of making sure I didn't wander off.

> One Liners
>
> "Did you have him sign it before he died?"

Fast forward to 2010 in Springfield, Ohio. My students were working on an assignment in class. My classroom was located in the rear of the building. The entire south side of the classroom was a series of windows. Looking out those windows you saw nothing but trees. I don't know what possessed me to do the following, but I did.

Out of nowhere I shouted, "Oh my God! There's a skyscootus!" The kids made a dash for the windows.

"What are you looking at?" one kid asked.

I said, "There's a skyscootus out there."

"What's a skyscootus?" another student questioned.

I said, "Well they are difficult to describe. It is a mix between a bird and a squirrel. They're very tough to spot because they can camouflage themselves."

"There it is! It just jumped from that big tree to the little one." I said.

After about five minutes, the kids returned to their seats.

They asked me how do you spell "skyscootus". They began to google it.

Password

I thought I had seen it all. Those of you who are old enough to remember the game show "Password", understand how the game works. As a source of review sometimes we played "Password". I was the host, Allen Ludden. The winning team stays for the next game. The losing team is replaced with two other competitors. We were in the middle of the game and I hear this beeping noise.
I said, "What's that?"

One of the girls playing the game reached down her blouse and pulled out her cell phone.

She said, "That's just a reminder to take my birth control medicine."

One Liners

"What was the name of the Wendy's girl?"

She didn't bat an eye and returned the the phone to its original position. Times have changed.

Pictionary

When completing a lesson, sometime as a means of review I played a form of Pictionary. The lesson being taught dealt

> ### One Liners
>
> "My aunt married my uncle."

with the situational advantages the white man had over the indians.

I printed the word "revolver" on an index card. I asked for volunteers to participate. Many hands went up and I picked a student at random.

I showed this young lady the card and she began to draw a picture of a revolver on the board. The kids were allowed to make a guess at any time. I noticed the drawing started to take a questionable shape. Many kids began to giggle. At the conclusion of the drawing, I asked this student to step back with me and admire her artwork. She was very embarrassed, but was laughing. Funny stuff! I continued to play Pictionary, but chose my topics a little more carefully.

Short Answers

How can you tell who the Major League scouts are at a baseball game?
Correct Answer: radar guns
Student Answer: "They're the ones with the radiator guns."

Hooky

From 1981 to 1984, I taught 7th and 8th grade at a parochial school. A young man played hooky for three days. His older brother covered for him at school. When we put two and two together, they were in deep doggie-doo.

Our principal did not believe in corporal punishment, so cracks were off the table. The mother of the two boys came to school and requested both of her sons be cracked. The problem was she wanted me to do it. I wasn't crazy about the idea, but I agreed to carry out her request.
I instructed the boys to take everything out of their back pockets and make sure they didn't move. I positioned the brothers facing each other with their hands flat on a desk. I applied three cracks to each boy and split the board on the final crack.

I enjoyed absolutely nothing about this experience. This was the only time I have ever cracked a student. Thank God!

Thirty years after the incident I ran into one of the brothers. He told me that day put his life on the straight and narrow. He is happily married with two kids and has a good job.

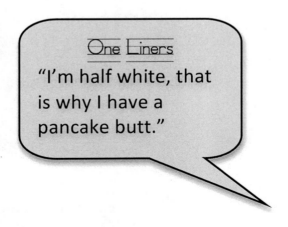

One Liners

"I'm half white, that is why I have a pancake butt."

Jo Jo

Cassidy Jo wasn't feeling well one day during her kindergarten year. In fact, she threw up in the cafeteria. She was sent to the nurse's office. The stomach flu was going around school. When Jo Jo entered the nurse's office it was packed with sick children. The nurse instructed Jo Jo to wait outside. A half hour had passed and things began to thin out in the office. The nurse went to get Jo Jo in the hallway, but she

"Just doing what I was told."

wasn't there. They searched the entire building and couldn't locate this little sweetheart. The principal ordered a "lockdown" and the authorities were called along with Jo Jo's mother.

This story has a happy ending. Jo Jo was exactly where the nurse had told her to wait ... "Outside". She was in a shelter house. Beautiful!

One Liners

"A fly pukes on you every time you try to move it."

Gene Yontz

Being a Student at St. Raphael in the 1960's

First kid in second row. I have the big ears.

Attended 8:00am mass Monday through Friday before school.
9:00am school began.
Wore white shirt and tie everyday.
Could not talk during lunch.
Religion class was held everyday.
Went to confession once a month (there were times I made up things I didn't do).
Walked to and from school grades 1 through 4.
Had to hold textbook at a certain angle (knuckles were cracked – Sister Agnes Bernadette).
Served mass whenever needed.

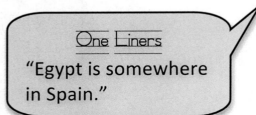

One Liners

"Egypt is somewhere in Spain."

When folding hands in praying position/right thumb over left.

> ### Short Answers
> What is another name for Lou Gehrig's disease?
> Correct Answer: ALS
> Student Answer: "LSD"

My First Day at CCHS

I went to Catholic Central High School in Springfield, Ohio. I was nervous and curious as was every other fifteen-year-old in 1968.

I picked up my schedule in the main office and hurried to homeroom. After the teacher took attendance, announcements began over the PA. I received three demerits for talking during announcements. I hadn't even been to an academic class yet. Those were the only demerits I received in my entire high school career. The teacher made an example out of me, which I incorporated into my disciplinary strategy. Start tough, you can always lighten up.

Hay is for Horses

In 1968, I was in the 8th grade at St. Raphael. Sister Mary Anina was my teacher. At the end of a Friday, one of the kids was misbehaving.

Gene Yontz

She shouted, "Hey!" directed at that student.

I opened my big mouth and said "Hay is for horses."

Sister replied "Mr. Yontz, you will be staying after school for that comment."

One Liners
"They're married together."

I asked, "Can I call my mom for a ride home?"

"Make it snappy," she replied.

I returned to class and Sister wanted to know what my mom had to say.

My mom said, "Have a nice walk home."

It was 4.6 miles in the winter. Lesson learned.

B+

I was very fortunate to be the father of two very smart kids with a great work ethic. Nick and Ashley were both members of the National Honor Society. Also, they were both in the top ten of their graduating class.

During Ashley's high school career, she received a B+ in an art class. All of her other grades were A's. My daughter is a perfectionist. She was a little annoyed with the B+, but not upset.

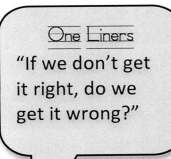

One Liners

"If we don't get it right, do we get it wrong?"

I said to her, "Don't worry about it too much, I received a B+ in high school."

She replied, "Yeah dad, but that was one of your good grades."

She was right.

Ashley had at least a 4.0 GPA every year. I also had a 4.0 GPA, but it took me two years to accumulate it.

What Are the Chances?

When I was attending Ohio Dominican College, one of my good friends Craig Raagas told me a story about a guy he went to Notre Dame High School with in Sherman Oaks, California. I told Craig that sounds like a guy I went to grade school with at St. Raphael in Springfield, Ohio. His name was Mike.

After many years, I sent Craig a picture of our 8th grade baseball team at St. Raphael. Mike was in the picture. Craig called and told me it was the same guy.

What are the chances that a guy I went to grade school with in Springfield, Ohio moved 2,500 miles away to California and ended up in the same high school with a great college friend of mine?!

Gene Yontz

SPORTS

Centerfield

I was seventeen and playing summer league baseball for WBLY. It was Memorial Day weekend and we were playing a Cincinnati team at the old Municipal Stadium in Springfield, Ohio. I started in centerfield, a position I normally didn't play.

I will cut to the chase. The Cincinnati team had the bases loaded. There was a shot hit over my head. I turned immediately and sprinted toward the fence. My leftfielder was telling me I had "plenty of room". The ball, my glove, and the fence all came together at the same time. Bottom line, the bar at the top of the fence jarred my glove from my hand. My glove landed over the fence with the ball in it. Grand Slam!
The embarrassing part was I had to climb over the fence to get my glove. When I returned, I looked over at my leftfielder and he had his glove up to his face laughing his butt off. I believe that was the final time I played in the outfield.

Short Answers

Who was the first woman appointed to the Supreme Court?
Correct Answer: Sandra Day O'Connor
Student Answer: "Sandra Day O'Hama"

Left or Right

I was a golf coach at a high school during the 1990's. Girls were allowed to play on the boys team if there were no girls team. During tryouts a young lady was complaining about her driving the golf ball.

I said, "Maybe it's the tee you are using?"

"What do you mean?" she asked.

I said, "Are you using the left or right handed tees?"
In the meantime, I sent a player into the pro shop with a Sharpie. He put a "L" and "R" on some of the plastic bags that contained tees.

I gave this girl a dollar to purchase the tees of her choice. She went to the pro shop and bought two bags of left handed tees. I came clean with her. She laughed and was a great sport. We are friends to this day.

My Favorite Umpire

I was the baseball coach at Catholic Central High School in 1983. Two of my players were brothers and lived with their dad and aunt. Their aunt was a nun, Sister Theresina. She was 4'9", old school disciplinarian and full of fire. Sister attended many of the home games.

Games during the week didn't start until 5:00pm because many of the umpires worked until 4:00pm. At this particular game we had the pleasure of having Amos Fitzwater behind the plate. He was a favorite around the county. Amos enjoyed his chewing tobacco during the game.

Sister Theresina sat in the second row on the first base side, very close to home plate. Her nephew, Gerald, was at the plate. He took a few pitches and swung at the next. The ball was foul-tipped into the ground and bounced up and hit Amos in the private parts.

One Liners

"Just go straight and follow the curve."

Amos screamed, "Oh s...!" while swallowing some tobacco juice. After hopping around for a couple minutes like he was on a pogo stick, Amos turned to Sister Theresina and said, "I'm sorry."

She replied, "Someone needs to go to confession."

Friday Night in Miami

Between 1972 and 1974, I attended Indian River Community College in Fort Pierce, Florida. I was awarded a baseball scholarship that Mr. Guenther helped me acquire.

We were in a very competitive league with the likes of Miami Dade North and South, Broward Community College, and Edison Community College. Most of the teams on our schedule were south of Fort Pierce. There were many outstanding players in the league that later became professionals. I was not one of them. I'm going to tell you about one of those players who became a Hall of Famer.

Gene Yontz

It was Friday night in Miami and game time was 7:00pm. I was on the hill that night facing the #2 ranked team in the country. Before the game, I intently watched Miami Dade North take batting practice. One good hitter after another took their cuts. I was quite impressed! Then "He"

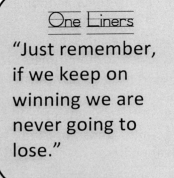

One Liners

"Just remember, if we keep on winning we are never going to lose."

entered the cage. What a stud! I quickly inquired who was this guy. At that moment I thought to myself, I'm going to remember the name.

There were only two things I recall about that evening in Miami. It was a beautiful night and Andre Dawson hit a home run against me that is still going. He didn't just hit the ball over the centerfield wall, but over the trees behind the wall.

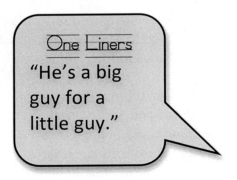

One Liners

"He's a big guy for a little guy."

Reds Game

Twenty-two years after "The Catch."

It was the fourth of May, 1991. The Cardinals were playing the Reds at Riverfront Stadium. Nick, Ashley, my wife and I had a room in downtown Cincinnati. It was a Saturday evening and Beach Boys night.

Ashley and Nick were five and six years old. The game started at 7:10pm. We were deliberating about what time to leave the hotel. We weren't sure how long the kids would hold up with the concert after the game. We bit the bullet and headed to Riverfront on foot. We made it in plenty of time for the first pitch.

Our seats were down the left field line in fair territory. The "green" seats at Riverfront. The Cardinals did not score in the first. Reds turn. Barry Larkin was batting third in the lineup. He ripped a line drive towards us. I've played enough baseball that I could tell the ball was headed for me. I didn't have much time to react. Nick was sitting to my right. I reached up and snagged that homerun ball with my bare hands above Nick's head. I received a round of applause along with a few complimentary beers from fans. I am thankful we decided to go to the game when we did. Otherwise I wouldn't have this great memory. Beach Boys were also fun!

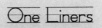

One Liners

"Todd's dad's girlfriend's uncle's daughter."

The S.B.L.

Many good times!

2018 Inductee into the Ohio Basketball HOF

On Sunday mornings during the winter months we played pick-up basketball. Many of the games were played in the friendly confines of CCHS gymnasium (now Jason Collier gymnasium). Dean Morgan, an instructor at the school had access to the building. Game time was 10:00am.

Most of the players were single and in their twenties. Mike Lyons, the commissioner of the league, named the teams. Each one of us were named after a current or former player. The roster of the Sunday Basketball League is as follows:

<u>Nuclear Health Spa</u>

6'0" Bill Brugger	"Hondo" Havlivcek	St. Bernard
5'11" Phil Brugger	Earl the Pearl	St. Joseph
5'9" Carl Bumgarner	The Matador	St. Bernard
6'0" Dan Lacey	Henry Finkel	St. Joseph
5'11" Mike Lyons	Bobby Jo Hooper	St. Bernard
5'10" Gene Yontz	Rudy Waterman	St. Raphael
5'9" Tim Malone	Doug Harris	St. Mary

Gene Yontz

<u>Vitalis All Stars</u>

5'8"Dean Morgan	Clyde Frazier	St. Mary
5'10"Marty Reibold	Glendin Torain	Franklin
6'2"Dan Schutte	Granville Waiters	St. Bernard
5'10"Joe "Pinto" Wickham	Special "K"	St. Raphael
5'10"Randy Yontz	Don May	St. Raphael
5'9"Ed ONeill	John Rinka	St. Teresa

Pat Day

My daughter and Pat Day at Churchill Downs

I love thoroughbred horse racing. I got the bug at the age of sixteen, thanks to my uncle in Louisville, Kentucky. Over the years I became a big admirer of the jockey Pat Day. To me, he was the "Michael Jordan" of horse racing.

In 2001, I was recovering from surgery due to cancer. I was laid up with a lot of idle time. My mom always told me that the answer is always "no" if you don't ask. I decided to write Mr. Day and ask if there was any way we could meet for lunch sometime. I addressed the letter to Churchill Downs. A few months later my phone rang around 6:00pm on a weekday night. I answered it and Mr. Day was on the other end.

One Liners

"Lemon juice takes freckles away."

I said, "Thanks for calling Mr. Day."

He replied, "Call me Pat. Mr. Day was my dad."

We talked about ten minutes and he invited me down to Louisville for lunch at Mitchell's Fish Market at the Summit. He told me to bring anyone I wanted and we would meet at noon. So, Nick Ashley and I made the three-hour trip just after Christmas.

Mr. Day was as gracious as could be. He spent three hours with us, allowing us to ask any question about any topic. He signed many items that I brought. Many pictures were taken which I cherish! We had such a great time!

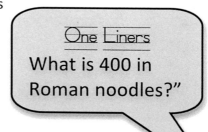

One Liners

What is 400 in Roman noodles?"

I was very humbled that Mr. Day would take time out of his busy schedule to spend time with us. This was a top ten

"Day". I still see Mr. Day once a year at Keeneland for a jockey signing to benefit the Permanently Disabled Jockey Fund. Such a nice man!

In a related story, I found a $100 bill at Churchill Downs. I've always wanted to know what it felt like to bet $100 on a race. I am generally a two and four dollar bettor. I decided to bet the $100 bill on a horse that Mr. Day was riding. The horse's name was "Highpoint". I hated the feeling of betting that kind of money on a horse race and it wasn't even my money. The horse did win and I received $230 in return. I will never do that again!

The Colosseum

Present Day Colosseum with no hoop.

The Colosseum is a 33' x 33' slab of concrete with a basketball hoop, located at 2217 Stowe Drive in Springfield, Ohio. This sacred structure was built in 1964, but didn't receive its name until 1966. Most of the games were played three-on-three any time of year weather permitting. All games had to be completed by 10:00pm. (Dad's bedtime. Lights were turned off.) Below are the individuals who have had the privilege of playing at the Colosseum:

'69 Gary Bumgarner
'69 Jim Connors
'69 Steve Connors
'68 Jack Conroy
'69 Tom Dingledein
'69 Jim Donahue
'72 Joe Donahue
'69 Doug Drennen
'72 Dennis Elix
'72 Dick Fuller
'69 Dave Hilbert
'67 Joe Kunkel
'68 Tim Kuss
'72 Dave Legge
'72 Dave McGuff
'73 Doug Montanus
'69 Dean Morgan
'67 Mike Murphy
'69 Pat Murphy
'65 Gene Nevious
'69 Bill O'Neill
'69 Marty Parrill
'69 Larry Reeb
'69 Paul Skinner
'68 Steve Sutch

'69 Pat Szempruch
'65 Mike Ulliman
'68 Bob Vollmer
'72 Dennis Whalen
'69 Jerry Whalen
'74 Craig Yontz
'72 Geno Yontz
'69 Randy Yontz
'68 Rick Yontz
'80 Terry Yontz

All of the above are graduates of Catholic Central High School.

What is That?

I worked at Snyder Park Golf Course as seasonal help for six summers during high school and college. I was also the greens keeper from 1977-1981.

Sometime during my employment I recall seeing a very peculiar animal on the course. Between the seventh green and eighth tee, just off the cart path to the right was a ten-foot pine tree. Under that pine tree was an animal that had the face of a cat, but hopped around like a rabbit. We called it a "Cabbit". I don't know whatever happened to it, but it was very strange.

What an Idiot!

My workday at Snyder Park Golf Course began promptly at 6am and the maintenance gate was locked at 2:30pm on my way out. The greens were mowed first thing every day. Two riding mowers were used to mow nineteen greens, which included the putting green. This job took approximately two hours for each mower.

Short Answers

What are the Bill of Rights?
    Correct Answer: The first ten amendments.
    Student Answer: "The Ten Commandments"

> ### One Liners
>
> "Concerning my bucket list, I want to poke a dead body with a stick."

I was mowing the sixteenth green ... the last one assigned to me. I always removed the flagstick from the hole prior to mowing. I noticed a golfer about 150 yards out in the fairway. He must have started on the back nine, which was frowned upon. I was mowing the greens in a side to side direction. I kept my eye on this guy as he took many practice swings. He fired away while I was on my mower! The ball hit my leg on the fly and rolled to a part of the green that was not mowed. I was so angry! I mowed over that ball and shot it over the railroad tracks. If you have ever played Snyder Park, you know where I am referring. That dude didn't even approach the green. He moved on to the next tee. What an idiot!

Two Tickets

The following took place in Lafayette, Indiana at Tippecanoe Junior High School. Two rather large male teachers agreed to wrestle each other to raise money for a local charity. They were decked out in leotards, capes, masks ... the whole mess. Each student paid fifty cents for admission. Mr. Russell, a teacher at the school, asked Steve, a student, if he was excited about the wrestling match.

Steve said, "Yes I am Mr. Russell. I even bought two tickets." Mr. Russell asked, "Why did you buy two tickets?"

Steve replied, "In case I lose one."

Mr. Russell thought that was a little different. Steve proceeded to reach down his sock and pulled out both tickets. They were stapled together!

Buzzer Beater

I coached girl's basketball for fifteen years at many levels. The most talented player I had the privilege to coach was a young lady, Amanda Wood. She was a five-foot seven-inch post player in high school. Obviously, not tall for that position.

We were playing on the road at Northeastern. Amanda made my assistant aware that she had forgotten her sports bra. We tried to contact her parents, but our efforts were unsuccessful. We had to improvise. We found a few rolls of pro-wrap and passed them onto Amanda. She took it upon herself to solve the problem, if you know what I mean.

We were in the midst of one of our worst games. Nothing was working. We found ourselves down by two with five seconds to go. We had the ball out of bounds under the Jets' basket. We practiced a play weekly called "Fire", which was designed to travel the length of the floor in a few seconds. The ball was entered to Amanda. After a couple of screens and four hard dribbles, Amanda crossed midcourt and she let it fly. The ball rattled around and fell in. We win by one with the "support" of pro-wrap.

Playing Time

A friend of mine was head coach of a girl's high school basketball team. Some of the parents had been complaining about the lack of playing time for their daughters.

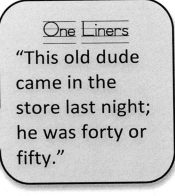

One Liners

"This old dude came in the store last night; he was forty or fifty."

The final home game of the season had arrived. The coach sent eight players out on the floor for the opening jump ball. The referee instructed the coach he could only play five players at a time. The coach turned toward the parents and said "See, I told you. You can only play five at a time." Coach had guts.

Being a former coach, I love that story.

The Memorial

The Memorial golf tournament is held at Muirfield Village in Dublin, Ohio. A good friend of mine and my cousin were in attendance. It was a hot, humid day in late May and both had been frequenting the beer tent. My friend Doug had to relieve himself. He chose a porta-potty in an isolated area on the course. While he was going pee-pee, my cousin knocked on the door and said, "Doug, Payne Stewart is out here and he has to go."

Doug said, "You can tell Payne Stewart to kiss my a**."

My cousin replied, "No Doug. He is really out here."

Doug replied, "Well he is just going to have to wait."

When Doug was finished he opened the door and there stood Payne Stewart. About one hundred people had gathered and gave Doug a round of applause.

Payne said, "Sorry buddy, I really have to go."

The Golden Boy

In 1984, Matt was the quarterback at Catholic Central High School. He was an outstanding student, well mannered, and came from a very nice family.

After a two-a-day practice in August, two of the coaches were hungry so they each gave Matt a twenty-dollar bill to get them something from Wendy's. The coaches didn't realize the other one had given Matt money, so Matt had forty dollars in his possession. Matt and his buddies saw an opportunity to fill their bellies before returning to the fieldhouse. They wolfed down a bunch of food and threw some change in a bag and kept a twenty for themselves.

One Liners

A student was giving me his sales pitch for Kirby sweepers. "It's bulletproof and it can even spray paint your car."

Short Answers
What states have you been to outside of
Ohio?
    Student Answer: "Kentucky, Michigan,
    and Toledo."

The coaches finally caught up with The Golden Boy and his buddies. As punishment for his action, Matt was summoned to the football field on Saturday morning to wash, wax, and detail Mr. O'Neill's blue Chevy Camaro. The Golden Boy is now my insurance agent. Maybe I should check my invoice a little more carefully.

Wrong Way Mike

Mike was a member of the freshman basketball team that was coached by Fred Martin. The time period was 1979-1980. This was back in the day when each half started with a jump ball. By the title of the story, you can make a good guess of what happened. At the beginning of the second half, Mike received the jump ball and proceeded to make a lay-up at the opponent's basket. Coach Martin was not a happy camper. I believe the clipboard was split into many pieces.

Today Mike is fifty-two years old and Fred is sixty-eight. They are good friends and play a lot of golf together.

Gene Yontz

Career Change

I was the greenskeeper at Snyder Park Golf Course from 1977 to 1980. The following story contributed to me making a career change.

It was about midnight on a Saturday night and I was returning home from a night out. When I entered my apartment the telephone was ringing. It was ADT notifying me that there had been a break-in at Reid Park restaurant. I was on call for both courses that weekend, so I responded.

When I arrived at Reid Park it was pouring down rain. Someone had cut a hole in the roof of the restaurant to gain access. I called one of our employees to meet me at the course to repair the roof. The police also joined us.

The course was opening up for play in six hours. We had to work fast. The hole was repaired and covered quickly. I went up on the roof to check it out. Everything was in order, but there was one problem. Everyone had left the premises and took the ladder with them.

One Liners

"Mr. Yontz, I know you're a teacher and you're supposed to lie to us."

It's now 2:00am, pouring down rain. I'm on top of this roof, pitch black and no ladder. Not a good situation. I ended up positioning myself on the roof hanging with both hands and dropping to the ground. Hello teaching career!

Jim Tressel

My brother Terry passed on March 8, 2006. He was only forty-three years old. It was a very long, painful, struggle with cancer. He was hospitalized at the James Cancer Center at The Ohio State University. The last month of Terry's life was most difficult. He lost the ability to speak. Any correspondence with Terry was through a pen and yellow tablet paper.

Prior to Terry's last month on earth, he was able to speak with clarity. There was one special day I will always remember. Terry's dentist graduated from OSU. He was also the person who detected a spot on Terry's tongue that looked suspicious and led to his diagnosis. Dr. Schanher had a few connections at OSU. He contacted Jim Tressel's secretary and explained Terry's situation.

It was on a Saturday afternoon around 5:00pm. I exited the elevator with Terry's daughter Rachel. We were headed to Terry's room and to our surprise Terry was walking in the hallway.

He said, "Guess what?"

I said "What's up?"

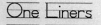

One Liners

"Isn't Hank Aaron the baseball player that has a disease named after him?"

He said with a big smile. "Jim Tressel just called me and we talked about ten minutes."

I replied, "That's awesome!"

I will always be thankful to Dr. Schanher and Jim Tressel.

That was the last time I saw Terry smile.

Call Me Coach

I have a wonderful niece named Katie. She is well educated with a degree from Miami University in Oxford, Ohio. Upon graduation from college she took a job with "Edwards Communities" as an event planner in Columbus. She was working a function which was raising money for a local charity. It was mostly a younger crowd attending the event. Katie noticed an older gentleman that seemed to be confused or out of place.

Katie approached him and asked, "Sir, may I help you?"

He responded, "Just call me coach."

Katie said, "Okay, where did you coach?"

Earl Bruce just turned and walked away. Go Bucks!

One Liners

"Did China have any electoral votes in the last election?"

<u>Short</u> <u>Answers</u>

What is performed to determine the cause of death?

Student Answer: All topsie

The Ultimate Team Player

The 1963 undefeated football team at Catholic Central was coached by Mickey Hannon. Some of the players on the 10-0 Tornadoes team included: Bobby Armentrout, Jimbo Meyer, Mike Moone, and Stan Erter. There was a relatively unknown sophomore who played a major role in the victory over Lima Catholic that year. He was not very tall and very skinny.

Over a half of a century ago, one of the starters had forgotten his cleats, both of them. He happened to be the quarterback, Bobby Armentrout. My hero, Mike Trempe, stepped up and passed his cleats onto the signal caller for the game. There are only a handful of people that know about this part in the history of the CCHS football program. Mike Trempe was the ultimate team player.

Mike later became a standout at Lenoir-Rhyne University in North Carolina. He is now a prominent individual in the Springfield community. The entire Catholic Central family says, "Thank you!"

Gene Yontz

Hammer Time

In 1982, I was a first year baseball coach at Catholic Central High School. We had seven seniors on our team which provided for a good nucleus.

We were playing for the sectional title against West Liberty Salem. My leadoff hitter was centerfielder Greg Vanvelzor. It was the bottom of the seventh inning and we were the home team. The score was tied 6-6. My number nine hitter led off the inning with a walk. Greg was next up. I thought about bunting the runner over to second, but decided to let Greg take his cuts. It was the best coaching decision I have ever made. Greg hammered a walk off home run over the left field fence. It was Greg's first home run in his life. A wild celebration took place at home plate. I still see Greg today. A great memory!

One Liners

"Remember that one day we talked about it two days straight?"

FAMILY AND FRIENDS

Hat Trick

In 2001, I was in the process of being released from the James Cancer Hospital at Ohio State University following surgery for prostate cancer. The surgery was very successful. Obviously I was delighted and thankful.

I entered the room and there were three men in white coats waiting on me. I didn't know how many of them were doctors, but I did recognize one of them. He was my surgeon. My surgeon put on his plastic glove and gave me my final evaluation.

> ### Short Answers
> Who is the all-time hit leader in Major League Baseball?
> **Student Answer:**
> Peat Rose

He said, "I hate to do this to you Mr. Yontz, but I need to have my intern do the same."

After round two, I looked at the third person in a white coat and said, "Don't even think about it. There is no hat trick going to happen here." Everyone laughed and I was released. I am still here seventeen years later. I am a lucky man!

Has This Ever Happened to You?

It was a cold, rainy, miserable night in September and I had stopped at a Speedway station to buy some refreshments. I think I purchased a twelve pack of "Coca-Cola". I returned to my black Toyota Camry and attempted to start my car. I looked up from my driver's seat and saw a guy waving his arms in the air and he said, "What's going on dude?"

I had gotten in the wrong car. Both of our cars were black and mid-size. After I exited his car I told him thanks for not shooting me.

Las Vegas Wedding

C.F. Martin and the bride.

I was headed to Las Vegas for three days with Fred over COTA day weekend. It was very crowded at the Columbus airport prior to boarding. A young lady had a garment bag draped over the seat next to her. I politely asked her if my friend could sit there. "Sure," she said.

Fred sat down and started up a conversation with this lady … as he always does. The garment bag contained her wedding dress. The couple were getting married at the Flamingo on Saturday afternoon at 4:00pm. We were staying at the Mirage across and down the street on

> One Liners
>
> A girl on our high school basketball team asked my assistant if he had any Midol. He said, "No. It makes me too moody."

the strip. Gary and Natalie invited us to stop by for the wedding if we wanted. So that's what we did. We got cleaned up and showed up. The bride and groom were surprised and thankful we stood up with them. Fred was a lovely Maid of Honor and I was a dashing Best Man. Our signatures are on the marriage certificate as witnesses. I have pictures.

Girlfriend in Columbus

A mode of transportation in the 1970's was hitch hiking. I was dating a girl in college from Columbus and didn't have any wheels. It was a Friday afternoon in the summer and I embarked on my hour trip to the state capital.
I was on a ramp in the south end of Springfield headed east on I-70. Two girls with a baby in the backseat offered me a ride. After entering the car, I realized they were buzzed.

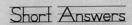

Short Answers

How do you spell "Jesus"?
Student Answer: Hey Zeus

They asked me if I wanted to smoke. Obviously, I told them no.

We arrived at the Grandview exit. They were headed left and I was going right, so I got out. I was about one mile from downtown. The plan was I would get to downtown and my girlfriend would pick me up. As I was walking from my drop off point, a car pulled over and a guy asked me if I needed a ride. He looked a little shady. Do I or don't I?

I said, "Okay, I'm just going downtown."
I entered the car and it wasn't more than a minute when this guy said, "There are a lot of gays in these bigger cities, and I'm one of them."
I tried to remain calm and said, "Just let me out right here."

One Liners

"If Russia attacked Turkey from behind, would Greece help?"

He pulled over and dropped me off without incident. That was the final time I stuck my thumb out.

Edie Takes a Tumble

This story was told to me by my mom, Edith Yontz. Mom had eight brothers and sisters and the time period was the early 1930's. She was born in 1928 and was five or six when the following occurred.

My grandfather was driving the car loaded with kids headed into Springfield from Summerford. At some point in the trip, mom fell out of the vehicle or was pushed out by her brother Jim. The interesting part of the story was no one told my grandfather for about three or four miles down the road in fear of getting blamed. Everything ended well with her dad turning around. Mom said the only thing she remembers is picking gravel out of her head. I asked her if she was scared. She doesn't remember, but she figured they would be back to get her. Uncle Jim is ninety-five and still denies the push.

Family Crest

I had never heard of a "Family Crest". I had no idea what it meant. Enter Eddie Griffin. Eddie was a high school friend and we grew old together. We were on a five-day bus trip to Boston with fifty senior citizens. It was September of 2016. Eddie was wearing a t-shirt with a symbol on it that represented his family's name.

Eddie asked, "What is the Yontz family crest?"

I replied, "I have no idea."

He said, "I bet your brother Randy knows."

I said, "He's right over there, go ask him."

Eddie returned laughing and shaking his head.

I said, "What did Randy have to say?"

Eddie said, "Randy told me the Yontz family crest was a can of Strohs."

Mom's Surgery

Granny and Caroline

My mom underwent surgery on her carotid artery. After surgery, she was placed in "intensive care". I would stop and see mom each day. I was required to stop at the nurse's desk to check in before entering her room. This procedure occurred daily. After several days of visiting mom, the nurse told me that I no longer had to stop at her desk. I began to bypass the nurse's station and entered my mom's room.

One Liners

"Our high school is more high tech, but they're back in the past."

This particular day I visited mom, there was no nurse in the room. Mom was sleeping and I didn't want to wake her. I went home and called my brother Craig that night. He told me the same thing happened to him on his visit to mom.

The next day I went to see mom. I entered the room and there was a nurse present. I asked her, "Is mom doing okay?"

She said, "Oh Mr. Yontz, that's not your mom. She was moved to another room two days ago."

The lady in the bed looked exactly like my mom with her hair pulled back.

I did tell mom about this, she just laughed. Embarrassing!

A Great Day

Ashley and Nick were born three hundred and sixty-three days apart.

Nick was little and at the point where he could move around the room holding on to sofas and chairs. He was not quite sure of himself taking steps without assistance.

The day after Ashley came into the world, Nick and I visited her in the hospital. I remember we arrived in the afternoon and spent a few minutes in the waiting room to see Ashley. A nurse came in and told us we could go in.

I said, "Come on Nick, let's go see your baby sister."
At that moment, he let go of everything and took his first steps across the room. What a thrill! I will never forget it. I saw something that no one else in the world got to see. I am very proud of Nick and Ashley.

Aunt June

My Aunt June died in 1992 in Louisville, Kentucky. She enjoyed her beer, cards, and horse racing. We had a lot of fun together.

Many family members made the trip from Springfield to Louisville to pay their respects. It was a very nice ceremony. Upon leaving the funeral home, Aunt Donna and Craig were in the back seat. I was in the front and Sandy was driving.

Our destination was Sandy's residence. It was a quiet ride to Sandy's house, not much conversation until ...

Craig asked, "Where is June going to be buried?"

Sandy replied, "She's not."

Craig counters, "Where is she?"

Sandy said, "In the urn next to you."

Aunt Donna claims that if the car wasn't moving, Craig would have vacated the vehicle.

The Munsters

I have a cousin who drove a school bus for a local high school. This particular day, she was transporting the girl's soccer team to Graham High School. She dropped the team off near the entrance and proceeded to park the bus.

Game time was about an hour away. Nature was calling Pam, so she headed to the nearest restroom. As she was sitting there, she reached in her purse and pulled out chapstick and applied a heavy dose. After finishing her business, Pam walked around a bit to kill time. As it got closer to game time, she made her way to the bleachers.

The game is in the first half and Pam checks out her cute self with her compact. Mistakenly, she had applied her son's "eye black" not chapstick. Eye black is what some athletes spread under their eyes during competition. Pam could have landed a role in the "Munsters" with that look!

Gene Yontz

Beer Run

My cousin Jimmy lived on the Kentucky side of the Ohio River near Louisville. It was a Saturday night and the gang had run out of beer. It was too late to purchase beer in Kentucky.

Jimmy improvised. He fired up his boat and headed across the Ohio River to Indiana. He had two passengers, his mom and uncle. It was approximately 2:00am. On the beer run to Indiana, Amos, Jimmy's uncle, stood up in the back of the boat to relieve himself. When Jimmy saw this he made an abrupt turn tossing Amos in the river.

Everything turned out fine with nobody getting hurt. They did reach their destination. Mission accomplished!

A Dog Gone Good Day

I have a cousin who lives in Evansville, Indiana. His name is Terry. His dog "Mozzarella" had been missing for two days. No explanation why. Terry heard of an accident that involved a dog so he checked it out. Terry went to the scene of the accident and saw Mozzarella in the street. He wrapped Mozzarella in a blanket and gave him a proper burial on a farm that his friend owned.

One Liners

A girl said (referring to her jeans), "The hole in my butt is getting bigger."

A few days had passed and Terry heard some scratching and barking at the back door. He opened the door and it was Mozzarella. My cousin had buried the wrong dog. I don't know how that could happen, but it did.

Steak 'N Shake

In the 1980's, a friend of mine was an assistant high school basketball coach. He was returning home from a coaching clinic in Indiana with the varsity coach. They stopped at a Steak 'N Shake in Indianapolis and my friend ordered a hot fudge sundae.

The waitress asked, "Do you want your nuts crushed?"
My friend replied, "Do you want your b... pinched?"
Couldn't get away with that today!

<u>Short Answers</u>

What do you call parking services provided at restaurants and social functions?
   Student Answer: Ballet parking

Gene Yontz

Point and Laugh

A group of us teachers were headed to Myrtle Beach for a golf trip during spring break. It's a long nine-hour drive. There were eight of us in three vehicles.

I was a passenger in the third car sitting in the backseat. I was bored out of my mind. There is just so much reading a fellow can do.

I had an idea, so I ran it by the other two gentlemen in the car. After getting their approval, I put my plan in motion.
In the back window of the car I was in, I placed a sign made out of a large piece of cardboard that read, "Point and laugh at the blue car in front of us." About ten cars followed our instructions. It was hilarious!

Eventually, the driver of the blue car pulled over and got out to check the back of his vehicle. We also pulled over, and asked what was the problem. Mike thought we had put a bumper sticker on his car. I don't recommend doing this in the world today.

Short Answers

Where is the Medulla Oblongata?
Correct Answer: In the brain stem.
Student Answer: Africa.

The Drive-In

Mr. And Mrs. James Monroe

One of my friends shared his story with me. He was sixteen and just received his driver's license. He had his eye on this beautiful girl in class. She was fifteen, shy, and naïve. He summoned the courage and asked her out on a date, but didn't tell her they were going to the drive-in.

Date night had arrived. The boy picked up his date on time and headed to the movie. During the course of the date he began to make a few small advances. He began to kiss her with some positive response from his date. This smooth young man then slipped an eight track tape in. The song was "Let's Get It On" by Marvin Gaye. He was beginning to feel pretty confident about himself. His imagination started to get the best of him.

He said, "Do you want to get in the back seat?"

She replied, "No, I would rather stay up front with you."

They have been together over forty-five years.

Sorority House

Still standing on Fountain Ave.

I was in my mid-twenties and living with my brother Randy and a friend in the other half of a double my brother Rick and his wife Barb owned.

It was late on a Saturday night, and I returned home from a get together with friends. I entered the back door and turned on the lights.

"Turn out the lights! Turn out the lights!" my roommate screamed.

> ### One Liners
> I asked the class if anyone knew the Marines hymn. A girl said, "I think I do. Isn't that the one which starts out 'From the halls of Montezuma to the shores of Tennessee'?"

I assumed he was with a girl in inappropriate dress. I approached with extreme caution. When I entered the living room, I saw my roommate with his knees in the couch, carefully pulling apart the curtains. He was looking at the sorority house across the street.

I said, "What's going on?"

He replied, "Just checking things out across the street."

I said, "How long have you been watching?"

"About ten minutes. Here take a look," he said.

I can't give you any more details. End of story.

> ### One Liners
> I told a kid that he could lift a ton but couldn't spell it. He said, "I can too, T-U-N."

Victoria Secret

I was helping a friend work a baseball card show at a local mall. While talking with this friend, I noticed a Victoria Secret store located over his right shoulder. One of my former students happened to be working at this store and was in plain view.

One Liners

"When I was in the first grade, I received a sponge bath from the best looking nurse I've ever seen in my life."

I said to my friend, "I heard that if you ask a girl at a Victoria Secret store to model lingerie for you, she would." He didn't believe me, so I said, "Watch this."

I entered the Victoria Secret store and told the girl I was playing a joke on a friend. She was more than happy to play along. She pulled a sexy outfit off the rack and asked for my approval. I turned to my friend and gave him the okay sign that this was going to happen. Five minutes later she returned with the outfit, but not wearing it. We both turned and waved to my friend.

Coffee Pot

There was a power outage in the neighborhood that lasted for an extended period of time. A husband and wife team were forced to spend the night in a hotel. The wife had to work early in the morning, the husband did not. When the husband rolled out of bed, his wife was already at work. He proceeded to make a cup of coffee, but couldn't get the filter to fit into the coffee pot. He called his wife at work and explained his predicament. It turned out the wife had a problem with incontinence and left a panty-liner on the counter by mistake. The husband tried to use the panty-liner as the filter. I think it was Maxwell House, "good to the last drop".

Kidnapped

Amy and Kent Young

My dear friend, Kent Young, is the nicest man I have ever met. He is the "Salt of the Earth".

It was Friday night. Fred Martin and I traveled to Newlove Rd. and asked Amy, Kent's wife, if we could kidnap Kent for the evening. After getting her permission, we were on our way.

Fred was driving and we headed east on I-70 with no particular destination in mind. We got off at the Hilliard-Rome exit, proceeded to Trabue Rd and made a right. I had no idea where we were going but Fred did. He pulled into a gentleman's club parking lot. Kent immediately said "I'm not getting out of the car." Fred turned off the car and went to the front door. He returned shortly and we were off to find a place to eat.

We ended up at Outback Steakhouse. The three of us entered the restaurant at the same time. We sat at the bar while we waited for a table. Out of nowhere a biker chick approached Kent and asked him if he remembered her from a bike ride. She called him Joe.

Kent politely said, "Ma'am, I've never seen you before in my life."

She persisted with Kent and turned to Fred and said, "You were there too."

Things had turned strange. I didn't know what to think. Fred didn't have time to set all of this up. After a great night, we returned Kent to his beautiful wife.

One Liners

"What's that thing called when they drown you in the water?"

70

A beautiful home

1902 N. Fountain Blvd

I loved high school. It was one of my favorite times of life. A friend of mine was the last of six children. His parents were older and they would spend time in Florida. Doug was a junior and needed to finish high school. Leona, the family maid, would stay with Doug as a means of supervision. We always had a place to hang out when Doug's parents were in the Sunshine State. There were times I would go to Doug's house after school on Friday and return home on Sunday evening. Mom and dad didn't mind, at least they knew my location. There were many memorable moments at 1902. Some of which I cannot share, but this is one I can share.

Gene Yontz

In 1972, the hoop was attached to the garage

There was a small group of friends invited to the Fountain residence on a Friday night. A good time was had by all. The ladies went home and a few of the guys spent the night. Saturday morning rolled around and the guys began to get out of bed. There was one problem, we couldn't find Mike. We searched the entire house, nothing. We went outside and looked around. We found Mike. He was asleep on the roof of the garage behind the basketball hoop. He was okay, but he did have a little frost on him.

The Streaker

I was in my junior year at Ohio Dominican College in Columbus, Ohio. My residence was on the second floor in Fitzpatrick Hall. Fitzpatrick Hall was a co-ed dorm. The guys occupied floors two, three and four, the ladies five, six and

> One Liners
>
> "If a Catholic marries a Jew it is a sin."

seven. This was very convenient especially if you were dating a lady in the building.

It was a weeknight around 7:00pm. Most of the girls had returned from dinner hoping to study. Ohio Dominican was a "brainiac" school.

Four of us "gents" entered the elevator on the second floor and pushed button five. The elevator door opened and Mike took off sprinting down the hall with just his shoes and a mask. Girls were screaming and laughing all the way around the rectangular layout. When Mike was approaching the conclusion of his trip, we closed the elevator door before he could get on. Not to worry about Mike, he headed down the stairwell to his room. Mike did get some interesting looks the next day.

> One Liners
>
> "You're an Indian taker."

First Impressions

I was in attendance at Kenton Ridge High School for a boy's basketball game between Greenon and Kenton Ridge. It was a Friday night and the game was supposed to be a close one. I arrived early during the J.V. game to get a good seat.

As I'm watching the J.V. game, I notice the Kenton Ridge coach was constantly yelling at the officials. He was banging on the scorer's table and stomping his feet. I thought to myself, who is this guy acting like a jerk?

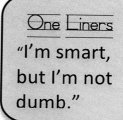

One Liners

"I'm smart, but I'm not dumb."

Fast forward four months. I was invited by a group of teachers to go on a Myrtle Beach golf trip over spring break in April. I accepted. Take a guess who was my roommate. Yep, the Kenton Ridge reserve basketball coach. I couldn't believe it.

After five rounds of golf, we became friends. To this day we are still good friends. His name is Fred Martin. The best way I can describe him is, he will do anything to you and for you. Cheers Fred!

Hee Haw

One Liners

"Did you know you can kill a donkey with a flaming hot dog?"

William Bradley Kincaid was an American folk singer and radio entertainer who still has major ties to Springfield. Bradley became a member of the Grand Ole Opry in 1935 and was inducted into the Nashville Songwriter's Hall of Fame in 1971.

In 1935, Bradley was working at WBZ-AM in Boston with Marshall Jones. Bradley commented that Marshall was always grumpy like a grandpa when coming into the studio in the morning for a broadcast. The nickname stuck and the rest is history. Bradley also gave Grandpa Jones the boots he wore on Hee Haw.

There were many times Grandpa Jones and Minnie Pearl visited Bradley at his home at 255 S. Bird Road. Bradley's son and grandson still live in Springfield.

Nicknames

Let's have some fun. Below are the nicknames of gentlemen from the Catholic Central High School Class of 1969. My brother, Randy, ran around with these guys. Your assignment is to match the real name with the nickname. Correct answers can be found at the end of the book. Don't peek! (Answers on page 86)

Gary Bumgarner	A. Tin Cup
Jim Conners	B. Peanut
Steve Conners	C. Buckwheat
Tommy Dingeldein	D. Fuzz
Jim Donahue	E. Dolph
Doug Drennen	F. Courtney Lips
Dave Hilbert	G. Fungus
Dean Morgan	H. Dumb
Billy O'Neill	I. Mouthy
Doug Skinner	J. Puttyman
Pat Szempruch	K. Spanky
Randy Yontz	L. Greasy Lou

Gene Yontz

1971 Beer Team

Undefeated!

In 1971 the drinking age for 3.2 beer was eighteen years old. Someone in the Class of 1971 at CCHS had a very creative idea. A beer team was formed and was comprised of Budweiser, Pabst, and Strohs consumers.

The Beer team had rules to follow just like any other team. There shall be no exercising. Each member must have one beer a day. Attendance was required at specific football and basketball games.

There were "official" members and "honorary" members. The official members received a purple shirt with white lettering. The honorary members were not issued a shirt because they were on an athletic team. I believe RECO sporting goods was credited with the production of the shirts.

I wonder how many of the original members still have their shirts. Jimmy Mann still has his shirt.

Gene Yontz

My Great Eight

Dad with his five boys in 1973

I could not have been born into a better family. I always felt important, safe, and loved. There were many sacrifices mom and dad made for us five boys. Dad worked two jobs for twenty years that enabled us to attend Catholic Central High School. He departed from 2217 Stowe Drive at 6:15am and returned at 6:00pm five days a week. Dad was a firm but fair man and absolutely would not tolerate any form of disrespect for mom. A heavy price was paid if this line was crossed. Dad lived for his five boys. There were many times I remember him saying "No partiality" and "Keep peace in the family". It was very important to him we were treated equally. The worst day of my life was the day after my dad passed. I woke up knowing I would never see him again. He was only fifty-nine. Please don't smoke!

Gene Yontz

I admire parents who are successful raising a large family. My mom was always the last one to bed and the first person to rise. She ran the day to day operations, but dad stepped in and put his foot down when needed. Sometimes he used both feet. Mom carted us around anywhere we needed to be. Mom believed in never being late. Two of mom's sayings were "And this too shall pass" and "The answer is always no, if you don't ask".

The Rick Yontz Family

Rick was the first of five boys born to Edith Mae Lyons and Kenneth Eugene Yontz. He is a 1968 graduate of CCHS, where he was Student Council President. He later became a "Golden Flash" at Kent State University. A KSU professor once told him he would never make it as an educator. Rick has been a teacher and principal for forty-four years. There was another person who had a question mark about Rick. It was Grandma Ethel. During Rick's college years, he returned to Springfield to work a summer job. After taking a shower, he would step in the hallway and shake his butt at Ethel. I was a witness to this on many occasions. He was wearing his underwear. Ethel would turn to me and say, "And he's going to be a teacher."

Recently Rick's kidneys failed and his son Brian gave a kidney and the gift of life to his father. Rick has been married to his wife Barb for forty-four years. They have two children Brian and Katie. Brian is married to Erin and they have 2 daughters, Claire and Caroline. Katie is married to Ted and they have a son, Teddy Jr.

All of the girls loved Randy, but he didn't seem to know it. Randy was and is a fashion plate, well dressed and well mannered.

Mom

When giving birth to Randy in November of 1950, mom was taken to the hospital in an army truck. It was the blizzard of 1950 and there weren't many vehicles on the road.

Randy is also a Kent State graduate and has enjoyed a successful forty-year career at the United Senior Services. He is very well thought of in the community.

Randy possesses a very good sense of humor. There is one establishment in Springfield where he is referred to as a "S*** Starter". He brings up a controversial topic for discussion and then fades into the background.

Randy's wife Teresa passed away in September of 2013. She was a saint! They have two wonderful children Michael and Maggie.

My brother Craig is a very interesting individual. He goes by "Butch", from Butch Cassidy and the Sundance Kid. My first memory of Craig occurred at 137 E. Southern Ave. He would lie in bed and sing the theme to "Lawman" before going to sleep.

Like myself, Craig is a graduate of Ohio Dominican University, a "brainiac" school. Butch was a good athlete but after a few knee surgeries, he went from the tennis court to the golf course.

There were many times Craig mentioned a guy named Spencer. For the longest time we thought Spencer was a fictional character. No family member had set eyes on him. It turns out Spencer did exist. He was Craig's wagering buddy from Columbus.

Butch moved around a lot. At one point when he was between houses, he moved in with mom at 2217 ½ Stowe

Drive. His stay was supposed to be for two weeks, but it lasted three years. I'm sure mom enjoyed the company.

Grandma Ethel opened my bedroom door on August 1, 1962 and said, "It's another boy." Terry had been born.

Terry was a very hardworking person who possessed a tremendous amount of self-discipline. I was visiting mom and dad one evening in October. They were watching the World Series and the Dodgers were playing. Terry, a big Dodgers fan, wasn't watching the game. He was in his bedroom studying for an important test the next day. Terry had a goal beginning his freshman year to be the valedictorian of his graduating class in 1980. He accomplished his goal. During Terry's address to his classmates, he stressed the importance of listening to your parents. It was a very proud moment for Mom and Dad.

When Terry passed in 2006 his youngest daughter Taylor was in the second grade. She is now a sophomore at Wittenberg University. Rachel is a physical education teacher at Reid School, and Casey and Tara were recently married.

Some things are unexplainable. Terry was in excellent shape. He ate right, ran, and didn't smoke. He was diagnosed with cancer and passed on March 8, 2006. He was forty-three. Sharee, Terry's fiancé, was a God send. She took care of Terry through some very difficult times. Thank you, Sharee.

Nick and Ashley at Pebble Beach

Nick and Ashley were born three hundred sixty-three days apart. Obviously they are the most important part of my life. Both received an award from the Daughters of the American Revolution in the eighth grade for good citizenship. They are members of the National Honor Society at Shawnee High School. They both have a degree with distinction from Ohio Northern University. Nick received his Master's degree from The Ohio State University and Ashley received her Master's degree from the University of Dayton.

I couldn't have been a luckier parent. I never worried about either one of my children making an unethical or immoral decision. I always felt in my heart they would do the right thing. I do worry about their health, happiness, and safety. When they are traveling, I have them send me a text when they have reached their destination safely. My only regret is

Nick and Ash never had the opportunity to meet my dad. Dad passed in 1984. Nick and Ash were born in the years after. My dad would have been so proud!

My most memorable moments of Nick and Ashley occurred at different points in their lives. Watching Nick take his first steps was very moving for me. Walking Ashley down the aisle to marry John was a thrill I will never forget.

Nick flies by the seat of his pants in his personal life. In his professional life, he is very much on top of things and pays attention to detail. Ashley's personal and professional life is lived by being organized and very regimented. She is a perfectionist.

I began writing this book on January 1, 2017. It has been a challenge and I am happy to complete an item on my bucket list. I hope you enjoyed the read.

Thank you very much!

Geno

Concerning your selection of the correct fictional story, email me at <u>derby2@att.net</u> and present your pick. I will get back with you regarding your answer.

Gene Yontz

Answers to Quiz on p. 75

G
A
C
H
F
I
D
B
L
K
J
E